Just Keep Blooming

Megan Mead

Presentation by *BookLeaf Publishing*

Web: www.bookleafpub.com

E-mail: info@bookleafpub.com

ISBN: 9789357740180

First edition 2023

*I would like to dedicate this book to God,
my lovely family, kindred spirits, friends
and everyone who has encouraged me on
this beautiful journey to embrace the world
of dreams and creativity.*

*And to everyone who needs this important
reminder:*

*You are blooming. You are special. You are
loved.*

ACKNOWLEDGEMENT

I would like to thank everyone at Book Leaf Publishing for their support and efforts throughout the making for this book. Also, a huge thank you to Lisa Robinson who helped with the design and artwork of the front cover. I am incredibly grateful for all of my family and friends, far and wide, who have inspired and encouraged me on this journey. Thank you for all of your love and encouragement.

PREFACE

Welcome to the 'Just Keep Blooming' family!

I am so glad you are here. I hope this book brings you peace and comfort.

Since I was a child, I have always loved to journal my thoughts on paper, expressing the lovely and challenging moments of each day. Over the years, this has led me to write poems as a form of relaxation and to encourage my imagination to be alive and free. I used to keep all of my poems to myself as an outlet to express emotions and memories in a personal way.

However, last year, I remember reading one of my poems to my amazing friend, Grace Hardingham, and from that moment on, I have never looked back. I didn't have any idea about the power one single poem could possess. Now, I write heartfelt songs on piano based on my poems and enjoy sharing what I have been given with others.

It is such a wonderful reality to realise that we have all been blessed with beautiful, unique gifts and talents to share with each other. So, I hope this book encourages you to embrace who are and find beauty where you are right now in your life.

Just keep blooming!

Love Meg x

P.S. I have always loved quotes since as long as I can remember, so…
Here is a collection of my favourite book quotes for you to enjoy:

"Dear old world, you are very lovely, and I'm glad to be alive in you'" - Anne of Green Gables

"It's not what the world holds for you, it's what you bring to it" - Anne of Avonlea

"If you look the right way, you can see that the whole world is a garden" - The Secret Garden

"Women don't just have hearts, they have souls and they have minds. They've got ambition and talent, as well as just beauty" - Little Women

"There is always something to be glad about" - Pollyanna

"Live your life like a Ghibli movie, where everything holds beauty and simple moments are adventures to be lived to their fullest" - Studio Ghibli

Where You Are

You are where you are,
Despite what others might utter,
Your journey is just beginning,
Living beyond word's chaotic clutter.

You are where you are,
Even when others may have found,
Their forever love and desire,
You have a beautiful smile, sacred sound.

You are where you are,
Just pause and gaze at the view,
Of who you are becoming,
You are blooming anew.

You are where you are,
Comparison is the thief of joy,
Hope is love's sunshine glow,
Darling, don't you know?

You are where you are,
The chapters are unfolding,
Like a moonlight in starlight sight,
There's always waiting and withholding.

You are where you are,
In this beautiful season,
So take in all its wonder,
For in a while, you'll ponder.

You are where you are,
Not in front, not behind,
Dreaming of what you find,
In time you will perfectly see,
That every moment is leading you,
To where you are meant to be.

Romanticise Life

Small simple moments,
Appear on our doorstep each day,
Travel to us on tomorrow's promise,
Beauty can be found come what may.

Ordinary views, normal sights,
Glimpses of sun's sweet gleam,
Robins flying past your window,
You live like you're in a dream.

Cups of teas, morning strolls,
Cosy evening of study and rest,
Time with friends and spontaneous fun,
All can be enjoyed for your best.

Look in wonder at little moments,
Bring joy to the mundane,
Grow roses out of weeds,
Love binds life, come sun or rain.

Tiny pieces of each day,
The plain, the good, the bad,
Woven into life's tapestry,
Romanticise life and be glad.

Book Moments

You are the main character,
With each seed that you sow,
Making dreams become reality,
With each page that you know.

You are the pen with hope to hold,
Chapters are turned by day,
Beautiful moments, fairytale dreams,
Like a beloved book of old.

Every moment of waking day,
Magical mystery within your grasp,
Power to scribble, draw and write,
Words are the love that you say.

Though books are made, kept and sold,
Rewritten, changed and imagined,
Pen's purpose writes paper palaces,
Your story is worth more than gold.

Book moments are alive and true,
Stories to be lived and told,
Binded in wonderful wild adventures,
And the person turning each page is you.

Fairytale

Gliding on feathers of fairytales,
Spinning and dancing on stars,
With eyes of beauty blissful,
Longing to somewhere find ours.

Amidst chaotic confusion,
Of world's changing cold,
With hope for sweet love's liberty,
In fields of glimmering gold.

A boy lost in his own warped ways,
A girl with joy, hurt and love,
Both collide in fairy gaze,
And meet like a sun kissed dove.

In storybooks of palace old,
Dancing in golden glaze,
Of sugar coated honey dreams,
With love and peace they daze.

Reading all these tales and stories,
Longing for this kind of life,
Where boy meets girl, love finds its way,
Our mind and hearts are led astray.

For life is full of pretty promises,
A red rose blooms not a moment too soon,
In the garden of our minds,
Hoping on sun and star and moon.

But life is full of sacred strife,
With heartache, pain, hurt and sorrow,
We persevere in our hopeful hearts,
For us to see our bloom tomorrow.

Each of us partakes in a story,
The novel of finding who we could be,
With each passing pain and glory,
We can dream and love and see.

To Wait to Love

To wait, to search, to wonder,
With hopeful, wishful mind,
To look, to gaze, to ponder,
As each day does unwind,

To love, to hope, to dream,
Beyond the here and now,
Yearning for a golden beam,
Of what could be life's vow.

All is part of your journey,
In each special season,
For every single moment,
Has purpose and radiant reason.

Waiting is a way of searching,
Through all the hurting and hoping,
Believing in what could be,
So wait, love beautifully and see.

What You Bring to this World

I've heard this saying,
From beloved book of old,
About a girl, a redhead,
Who lived for every sunset gold.

She claimed she loved each passing season,
No matter what did come,
And danced at graceful, gentle pace,
With purest love and reason.

The friends she made,
The joy she gave,
To the world and all she knew,
Meant that she could care,
Whilst in 'depths of despair'.

Her name was Anne Shirley,
She believed in bright tomorrows,
That love blooms over time,
Life is a beautiful complexion,
Of hopes and of sorrows.

She was a girl who realised,
What matters most of all,

Is what you bring to this world,
What you bring is you.

9

Kindred Spirits

Kindred spirits can be found,
Within each ray of sun kissed light,
Which caresses leaves that float and fly,
Autumn auburn in nocturnal night.

Beyond crowds and places of many,
Amongst rapid rivers of rain,
In this fallen wildflower world,
With all its hope, hurt and pain.

Someone who can see your sacred spirit,
And accept your faith led, fragile soul,
With gentleness grounding friendship,
No matter what is spoken or told.

One will soon be crossing your path,
Filled with fresh scented flowers and fun,
Dancing in this glorious garden,
Together, united, like moon and sun.

Kindred spirits can be sought,
Within each waking, sleeping season,
Begins a seed, becomes a rose,
Always there, and love is the reason.

Rose and Sun

I am just a little rose,
You are my sacred sun,
Beaming love's life giving light,
Even when I try and run.

Growing in Your golden grace,
Through all things take time,
Pretty promise in dryest place,
For I am Yours and you are mine.

Moments when I feel alone,
In this garden of sun and rain,
Some flowers discourage hope,
Causing hurt, doubt and pain.

Patient in spring's sweet bloom,
Yet frustrated in the waiting,
For flowers to bud and grow abide,
Faith through hope's hard chasing.

Knowing that You give me life,
The love I need to be,
Peace I find in lovely light,
Faith is garden's golden key.

To unlock my heart,
With these simple words,
I love you and will never fail,
My plans for you shall prevail.
For You are my rose and I am your Sun.

Imagination

A place we can all escape to,
When life becomes unclear,
In the midst of clutter's chaos,
We can bring joy ever near.

A pigment from our childhood,
Where we'd play and laugh all day,
Endlessly searching for colours and fun,
Until adulthood tried to take it away.

Chapters of fairytale lands and pages,
Palaces of peppermint sugar delight,
Sunshine gazing down onto the world,
Stars smiling at each other in the night.

Dreaming about wonder and peace,
Wishing on bright shooting star,
Trees dancing, horses prancing,
We can live in beauty where we are.

Our mind can truly come to life,
When we embrace our inner child,
Wherever we are, she is not very far,
So let imagination run free and wild.

Buried Hope

Sometimes hope is like a sandcastle,
Secure within its foundation,
Then sea waves lash against the shore,
Lapping life's hope for more.

Buried in hustle and bustle,
Of people's rule and regulation,
Darting between ocean and land,
Unable to hold hope's hand.

Sometimes hope is like a seed,
Planted in winter's soil,
Hidden away from sun's sight,
An finch's invisible first flight.

Buried only for a while,
Until it buds and blooms,
Into a sacred sunflower tall,
Light gleams through it all.

Hope is alive in every heart,
The sand strong, the soil slow,
Fragile finch, sunflower steady,
Hope blooms when she is ready.

Beautifully Blooming

I gazed in a ditsy daze,
At each sleeping creature and flower,
Eyes gently caressed and blessed,
Watching nature grow in a haze.

A ruby rose stood proud and strong,
Surrounded by scattered ferns and leaves,
Seeds gliding in September breeze,
Being rooted in soil where they belong.

I sat on a sturdy stone,
Overlooking lakes and tides,
Of how a plant can bloom,
Even when it grows alone.

In time I reached conclusion,
Each petal unfolds like a blushed heart,
Beautifully blooming day by day,
Not merely a fantastical illusion.

I gazed in meadows of seeds that sow,
Through each season, day and night
Wondering what I have yet to know,
Beautifully blooming as I live and grow.

Serendipity

I believe in sweet surprises,
Gliding on wings of reason,
Where each new day has a beginning,
Life has beauty in every season.

I believe in petal's promise,
That we are all unique,
Blossoming from seed to flower,
In every plan we make and seek.

I believe in hopeful happenings,
Woven within each ordinary day,
Painted, coloured and fully alive,
Fate opens up what life has to say.

I believe in mighty miracles,
Which showers earth one by one,
As rain dampens each patch of soil,
Faith grows fonder, with trust and wonder.

I believe in serendipity,
Seeds of life, sacred and bright,
For nothing is merely random chance,
Our purpose is love's pure light.

Soul

The soul which we are given,
Does not wither or age,
Although each day is new,
We are eager to turn the page.

From chapters still unwritten,
Filled with tide, turn and tear,
Wrapped in love, faith and grace,
We live for every sunshine year.

The soul does not crave for success,
Nor does she pine for wealth,
She abides in simple delights,
Like a music box on a shelf.

She tells us what is right and true,
No matter the risk or cost,
Protection from temptation,
Hope when we become weary or lost.

She smiles when we are kind,
Lifting our prayers into the air,
Floating on silver lined snowflakes,
Comforting those in deep despair.

The soul paints moonshine light,
Author of love and longing,
She guides her children to safety,
Giving them hope and belonging.

My soul is all of who I am,
She is my spirit from within,
Peace's paintbrush of life's purpose,
My soul is where I begin.

Song of Life

Life has different keys,
For shifting song and season,
All with promise, awe and wonder,
Played by heart's string and reason.

Summer grows major melody,
Sweet pea infused gardens,
Smiles and sun filled blessings,
Singing of hope's beautiful bloom.

Winter gives ice covered chords,
Change and snowdrop crotchets,
With sorrow and cloudy healing,
Played with minor feeling.

Peace is the piano,
Courage is the score,
Patience is the rhythm,
Love is life's core.

Beautifully Broken

Each and every piece,
Of pages torn apart,
Chapters changed, paper sealed,
Memories loved and lived in heart.

Broken pieces blowing the breeze,
Sweet salutations of sunset torn,
Rose tinted glasses of what could be,
With heart on sleeve and new book born.

Beauty in the petal pieces,
Broken, chipped and battered,
Heart of golden gloss and glass,
Bliss promised, torn and scattered.

Despite the loss of treasure trust,
Through days of love and pain,
Sunshine gleams on rose flushed heart,
After cleansing of the rain.

You see each piece of brokenness,
And every wishful pine,
Reminds you of your strength and smile,
A masterpiece being moulded in time.

Broken pieces have their place,
Carved together in love scented lace,
Heart beating in healing's pace,
Gloriously growing in time and grace.

Confidence

Confidence is a tiny seed,
Starting steady and small,
Growing with each passing day,
Hardly noticeable at all.

Confidence is a sunflower,
Blooming against the cold,
Brightening the way to live,
Despite what lies are told.

Confidence is free and blooming,
Like a cherry blossom tree,
Here to thrive and be content,
Planted for your heart to see.

Confidence is love's embrace,
When fear is sent far away.
Replaced with your radiant light,
Life is what you make it today.

Dancing Through Doubt

Dancing through doubt,
Leaping onto love's light,
Gazing at moon's smile,
Into the ebony night.

Singing in the rain,
Soaring above sky's storm,
Leaving fears and cares behind,
Waiting for each flower to be born.

Believing in the impossible,
Finding hope to grow and pray,
Knowing your gifts are made to share,
Sending insecurities far away.

Hoping in your heart's story,
Loving is what life is about,
Dreaming on painted starlight,
Dancing through doubt.

Laughter

Laughter is a sunflower
On a sunshine golden day,
Opening its honey petals,
No matter the storm in her way.

She lives in sweetened smiles,
Of friendship, love and delight,
Brightening a darkened room,
A star within the night.

Laughter is a medicine,
A remedy to life's sadness,
Light filling dimmed dreams,
Greeting people with gladness.

Awakening joy's slumber,
Dispelling weeds in hope's way,
Sunflower fields of smiles,
Spread a little laughter today.

Just Be And Rest

Hustling and bustling all around,
Searching frantically for the future,
Moving beyond the here and now,
Missing moments that could be found.
So just be and rest.

Busy beckons your everyday,
Sound dominant's sleepless nights,
Plans are made, kept and rewritten,
Life is given as gift, come what may.
So just be and rest.

Rest is receiving beautiful release,
In the soft sweet silence of today,
Corners of calm in rooms of loud,
Where heart's chasing does cease.
So just be and rest.

Loving life's journey at worst and best,
A miracle made to smile and bloom,
Through each season's sound and silence,
There's a waking flower called rest.
So just be and rest.

Remember

Remember, you are beautifully crafted,
Knitted and formed, wonderful and new,
No one is quite the same as you,
Weaved within world's wondrous canvas.

With gifts and talents to give and receive,
Voices to speak, ears to listen,
Life's garden sprouts come what may,
Dreams to live and achieve.

Comparison comes to prey and steal,
Lavender life and contentment,
Causing each flower to falter in growth,
Hope in honey that does heal.

Weeds take root in our mind,
When someone is unkind,
Beauty blurred in broken mirror,
Our eyes are blinded and cannot see.

You are wonderfully made,
Unique in earthly splendour,
There will never be another flower like you,
You are loved, chosen and true.

Remember, there is no need to compare,
Everyone has a precious path,
Woven and painted by the Creator,
Laced with love, planted with care.

Just Keep Blooming

Just keep blooming,
No matter what they say,
They may batter your mind,
With words untrue and unkind,
But they will learn someday,
So just keep blooming.

Just keep blooming,
Beyond the changing tide,
With storms and seas that stop and stare,
Each person who doesn't give a care,
You can live and love shall abide,
So just keep blooming.

Just keep blooming,
Growing in your heart,
With faith that floats,
Like beautiful boats,
In a calm chaotic abyss,
Everyone has a place to start,
So just keep blooming.

Just keep blooming,
Through every month and year,
The lessons you've learned,

The friends you've gained,
All are petals priceless,
From a daffodil dear,
So just keep blooming.

Just keep blooming,
Into who you are meant to be,
You will see in perfect time,
How beautiful you truly are,
Brighter than any star,
So just keep blooming.

www.ingramcontent.com/pod-product-compliance
Lightning Source LLC
La Vergne TN
LVHW010935200726
843509LV00013B/2227